THE LITTLE BOOK OF
IRELAND

Published in 2023 by OH!
An Imprint of Welbeck Non-Fiction Limited,
part of Welbeck Publishing Group.
Offices in: London – 20 Mortimer Street, London W1T 3JW
and Sydney – 205 Commonwealth Street, Surry Hills 2010
www.welbeckpublishing.com

ISBN 978-1-80069-399-9

Compiled and written by: Dave Verey
Editorial: Victoria Denne
Project manager: Russell Porter
Design: Tony Seddon
Production: Jess Brisley

A CIP catalogue record for this book is available from the British Library

Printed in China

10 9 8 7 6 5 4 3 2 1

Illustrations: Shutterstock

THE LITTLE BOOK OF

IRELAND

LAND OF SAINTS
AND SCHOLARS

CONTENTS

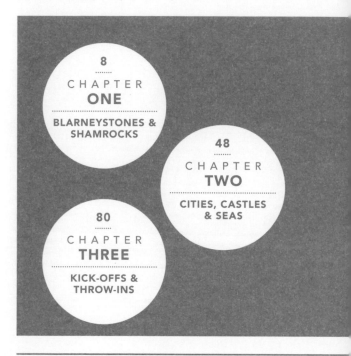

INTRODUCTION

CÉAD MÍLE FÁILTE – a hundred thousand welcomes!

To be clear, this book is about the whole of the Emerald Isle – encompassing both the Republic of Ireland in the south and Northern Ireland, which is part of the UK. There's a complex history there, no doubt, and yet today the Irish and the Northern Irish enjoy better relations than ever.

In fact, 10 million people a year cross oceans to visit this small island with a population half that. Some of them will tell you it's to experience a beer that tastes best at home, washing down some sweet-tongued blarney. Some come to invite the Irish muse to sit on their shoulder. Others to drive the green or change gears on a coastal road.

Sure, the Emerald Isle's green rolling hills, grassy pastures, deep valleys and pure waters help. And yes, it's expanses, dramatic wilderness and captivating peninsulas give way to cosmopolitan cities and inviting pubs, making it a bucket-list destination.

Where else can you cross a stone-arched bridge over a salmon-packed river to visit a lichen-spotted abbey? There's the jagged coastline of majestic sea cliffs inviting epic road trips through hidden-gem towns. There's castles, festivals, markets and music; geological flourishes, moody ruins and prehistoric monuments.

And that's before a song is sung, a boot is tapped, or even a mouthful of wild, foraged or farm-grown produce passes your lips. But when you leave? What you take with you: after the dramatic scenery, immense beauty and eye-watering landscapes remain tethered to Ireland?

The Irish people's warmth stays with you. If you get lost, they'll show you the way. If you're hungry and parched, they'll feed and water you. And if you fancy a yarn, God help you. It's a small, clean and green island, where a warm, engaging and feisty people have rolled out the welcome mat.

In the words of W. B. Yeats, "There are no strangers here; only friends you haven't met yet."

Chapter
ONE

Blarneystones & Shamrocks

Like a good Irish Whiskey,
the national character is complex and
smooth with a subtle sweetness.

There's so much to savour. Perhaps it's
best enjoyed like a 12-year-old single
malt... "Sipped in a small volume to let the
flavours be experienced."

The earliest confirmed inhabitants of Ireland were Mesolithic hunter-gatherers, who arrived sometime around 10,000 years ago. Signs of early agriculture, some 4,000 years later, saw the establishment of a Neolithic culture, evidence of which includes huge stone monuments and the oldest known field systems in the world.

The Romans referred to Ireland as Hibernia, it but was never part of the Roman Empire. Instead, a gradual blending of Celtic and indigenous cultures would result in the emergence of Gaelic culture by the 5th century.

Ireland is the third largest
island in Europe after Great
Britain and Iceland.

About the same size as Austria,
it has 3,171 kilometres
(1,970 miles) of coastline
and Carrauntoohil in
MacGillycuddy's Reeks is
its highest point, at
1,038 metres (3,405 feet).

"

I live in Ireland by choice, after experience of living many other places. Our neighbours are friendly, our view is beautiful, my political friends are fine upstanding people, my political enemies fascinating in their own way. I don't mind the gossip any more than the rain.

"

As quoted in Conor Cruise O'Brien's *States of Ireland*, 1972

Ireland's 300-mile length of
rocky outcrops, mountains,
forests, rivers and green fields
divided by hedgerows are all
ringed by sand dunes and
Europe's most scenic cliffs.

At just 170 miles across
at its widest, you're never far
from the sea.

"

When I was a kid, if you didn't
speak Irish, you really wanted to.
And you played Gaelic games and
you didn't pay any attention to
what was happening in the outside
world, because really, Ireland
was the centre of the universe.
And I don't think that's the case
anymore. Although, admittedly, it
is the centre of the universe.

"

Roddy Doyle

Ireland is surrounded by the Atlantic Ocean to its west, the Celtic Sea to the south, and the Irish Sea separating it from England to the east. These large bodies of water have a moderating influence on its climate.

> # The sea,
> ## the snotgreen sea, the scrotumtightening sea.

James Joyce, *Ulysses*, 1922

Ireland has a temperate
climate with warm summers
and mild winters. Rain
is common, but extreme
temperatures are rare.

Irish weather likes to keep you
guessing. You can experience
a little of everything, all in a
single day!

66

There's no bad
weather only
inappropriate
clothing.

99

Alfred Wainwright

Ireland is divided into four provinces roughly corresponding to the four cardinal points of the compass:

Ulster in the north
Leinster in the east
Munster in the south
Connacht in the west

Irelands largest cities are:

Dublin
Belfast
Cork
Limerick
Derry (Londonderry)
Galway

Derry / Londonderry

Ulster

Belfast

Connacht

Galway

Dublin

Lenister

Limerick

Munster

Cork

Each of the provinces is made up of
a number of counties:

Ulster
Antrim, Armagh, Cavan, Donegal,
Down, Fermanagh, Derry (Londonderry),
Monaghan and Tyrone

Leinster
Carlow, Dublin, Kildare, Kilkenny,
Laois, Longford, Louth, Meath, Offaly,
Westmeath, Wexford and Wicklow

Munster
Clare, Cork, Kerry, Limerick,
Tipperary and Waterford

Connacht
Galway, Leitrim, Mayo,
Roscommon and Sligo

"

The Irish is one race
of people for whom
psychoanalysis is no
use whatsoever.

"

Sigmund Freud

66

We Irish prefer embroideries to plain cloth. To us Irish, memory is a canvas – stretched , primed, and ready for painting on. We love the 'story' part of the word 'history', and we love it trimmed out with colour and drama, ribbons and bows. Listen to our tunes, observe a Celtic scroll: we always decorate our essence.

99

Frank Delaney, Irish novelist, journalist and broadcaster

Ireland's flat, low-lying area
in the midlands is ringed by
mountain ranges. There are glacier-
carved sandstone mountains,
rivers, lakes, sizeable inlets, islands,
peninsulas and tremendous
headlands.

The main river in Ireland is the
River Shannon, at 360.5km (224
miles) long. The MacGillycuddy's
Reeks of Kerry are the island's
highest mountains and include the
only three peaks over 1,000 metres.

Why the nickname "The Emerald Isle"?

Wherever you are on the island you will be surrounded by sumptuous shades of green… mint, forest, grass, pea, sea, olive… the list is endless.

With an abundance of countryside, luscious rolling hills, dramatic cliff tops, mountain peaks, grassy dunes, pleated cliffs and remote islands, Ireland is home to an astonishing hand of landforms and suites of colour.

66

The so-called Irish temperament is a mixture of flaming ego, hot temper, stubbornness, great personal charm and warmth, and a wit that shines through adversity. An irrepressible buoyancy, a vivacious spirit, a kindliness and tolerance for the common frailties of man.

99

Carl Wittke, historian

66

I'd never had any
problem finding
inspiration; Ireland was
always just there, you
know? All this richness
of culture was there
to tap into.

99

Brendan Gleeson , Irish actor

What is an Irish welcome?

Famously warm, multi-layered, elaborate and effusive. Expect a tidal wave of consideration upon entry to any Irish home complete with tea and fig rolls.

What is an Irish goodbye?

Brevity is not a natural gift of the Irish people, so, to shave hours off their journey, they'll edge towards the door without saying farewell to anybody.

Gone.

Ireland Natives

Red Fox: The largest of all the foxes

Irish Setter: A beloved breed with a
russed red coat

Connemara Pony: 14 hands high and
very gentle-natured

Pygmy Shrew: Ireland's smallest mammal

Irish Hare: Survived an Ice Age in the
south of Ireland

Red Deer: Ireland's largest land mammal

Pine Marten: One of the rarest mammals

The Viviparous Lizard: Ireland's
only native reptile

Hedgehogs, stoats, badgers and
otters are all common.

λ Religious People

Ireland is one of the most
Christian countries, with one of
the highest church attendances in
Europe — 34% of Ireland's citizens
attend church regularly.

Four out of five identify
as Christian.

78% identify as Roman Catholic.

Irish is Unique

Its names are magical and timeless, with meanings straight out of folktale:

Saoirse (seer-sha): freedom

Caoimhe (kee-va): dear or noble

Aoife (eefa): beauty

Fionnoula (finn-oola): fair-shouldered

Dáithí (dah-hee or daw-hee): agility or speed

Cara: friend

Ardál (ardal or awr-dahl): high valour

Aisling (ash-leen and ash-linn): dream or vision

Odhrán: dark-haired

The Blarney Stone

In County Cork, there's a block of carboniferous limestone that was built into the battlements of Blarney Castle in 1446 which is said to impart skill in flattery to anyone who kisses it.

However, a spot of work's involved. There are 128 narrow steps to climb up to it, then you've got to hang upside-down suspended over thin air to kiss the stone.

People who have kissed the Blarney Stone include:

Sir Winston Churchill

Stan Laurel

Ronald Reagan

Sir Walter Scott

Sir Mick Jagger

Kathcrine Jenkins

Eddie Redmayne

James Nesbitt

Joe Manganiello

The Shamrock

One of the national emblems of
Ireland and a symbol of good luck.
The druids considered it a sacred
plant, and myth has it Saint
Patrick converted a pagan king by
illustrating the holy trinity of the
Christian god with the humble
three-leaf clover.

"

Never iron a four-leaf clover, because you don't want to press your luck.

"

Irish proverb

Leprachauns

Small elves, maybe 3 feet tall, from Irish folklore, leprachauns are said to love gold coins, shamrocks, rainbows and anything green. According to legend, if a human succeeds in catching one of these little green men, it will grant you three wishes, or even give you its pot of gold. But they are tricksy, so have your wits about you…

"Where's my white out?"
"Chapter ten is missing!"
"Has anyone seen my socks?"
Linda spun around.
Mistress Yvonne gripped her
shoulders. "This is a regular
occurrence. No need to get
involved."
Faint shouts echoed down the
hall. "Leprechauns!"

Marlene Simonette, *Trouble in Bookland*, 2016

"

When anyone asks me about the Irish character, I say look at the trees. Maimed, stark and misshapen, but ferociously tenacious.

"

Edna O'Brien, Irish novelist, memoirist, playwright, poet and short-story writer

Did you know...?

Ireland has the highest number of
red-haired people per capita in
the world: 10%.

Ireland was the first country in
the world to legalize same-sex
marriage by referendum.

Trinity College

Is Ireland's oldest and most
prestigious university, founded
in 1592. It has educated many
of Ireland's greatest writers,
playwrights and poets, and counts
Irish presidents, Nobel laureates,
philosophers and mathematicians
among its alumni.

Walk through cobbled squares,
magnificent arches, wooden
doors and Doric columns to
the Book of Kells.

The Book of Kells

is a medieval hand-written devotional manuscript. Not only is it one of the finest examples of Celtic art, it is up there with the most beautiful documents in history. Lavishly illustrated and adorned, the original is displayed in a darkened shrine called the Treasury. Over 500,000 visitors a year queue to see this national monument.

Irish Proverbs 1

*Storytelling + human nature + humour
= Irish proverbs.*

It's easy to halve the potato where there's love.

You've got to do your own growing, no matter how tall your father was.

Don't be breaking your shin on a stool that's not in your way.

You'll never plough a field by turning it over in your mind.

Irish Proverbs 2

There's no use boiling your cabbage twice.

A trout in the pot is better than a
salmon in the sea.

Any man can lose his hat in a fairy wind.

Many a ship is lost within sight of
the harbour.

A friend's eye is a good mirror.

Irish Inventions

Colour Photography

Trans-Atlantic Calls

A Cure for Leprosy

The Modern Tractor

The Submarine

The Tank

The Guided Missile

The Ejector Seat

Whisky Distilling

Guinness

The Guided Torpedo

The Hypodermic Syringe

The Binaural Stethoscope

The Induction Coil

The Bacon Rasher

The Cream Cracker

Flavoured Potato Crisps

"

Dance as if no one
were watching,

Sing as if no one were
listening,

And live every day as if
it were your last.

"

Irish proverb

Chapter
TWO

Cities, Castles & Seas

Ireland's heritage towns are saturated in stories of the past – just ask any local and they'll regale you with all sorts of fantastic folklore.

Dublin

Ireland's famous capital is a coastal city
on the River Liffey, known for its friendly
welcome and long literary tradition.
Dublin is close to beaches, hills,
waterfront walks and trails.

A vibrant café culture and several
Michelin-starred restaurants have grown
among the city's storied public houses.

“

I go off to Dublin
and two days later
I'm spotted walking
by the Liffey with a
whole bunch of
new friends.

”

Ron Wood

If it's culture you're after, Dublin is home to the National Gallery, the Museum of Literature, the Museum of Modern Art, the Gaiety and Abbey Theatres and the National Concert Hall.

The 3Arena and the Bord Gáis Energy Theatre host international artists and shows.

International Rugby is played at the Aviva Stadium.

The Guinness Storehouse

A pint of plain. Black Custard.
Irish Champagne. Black bull drink.
Dublin mudslide.

☘

Guinness is Ireland's most famous
export and so, unsurprisingly
perhaps, its home is its most visited
tourist attraction. After seven floors
of ingredients, history and culture,
it all ends at the rooftop bar.

Dublin To-Do List...

Walk around **Phoenix Park**, the largest park in any capital city in Europe.

Take a pew at **Temple Bar**, serving up its unique mix of beer, whiskey, food, tunes and banter since 1840.

Take a **literary tour** to discover the touchstones of Dublin's famous writers – think Oscar Wilde, Samuel Beckett, James Joyce and Bram Stoker.

66

I live in Dublin, God knows why. There are a great many more congenial places I could have settled in – Italy, France, Manhattan – but I like the climate here, and Irish light seems to be essential for me and for my writing.

99

John Banville , Irish novelist

Galway

A Bohemian cultural city on the west coast, with beaches, a promenade and a buzzing city centre.

Labyrinthine cobbled streets host brightly painted pubs and a pedestrian artery packed with buskers, live music and street theatre, plus a cathedral, churches, Latin quarter, museum, castle and bridges over the River Corrib.

Derry

Derry is not only one of the finest examples of a walled city in Europe, it's the only in Ireland that remains completely intact.

It was built between between 1613 and 1618, to protect the new English and Scottish settlers from attack, having moved to Ireland as part of the Plantation of Ulster.

Killarney

Chock-full of sublime scenery: lakes, waterfalls and woodland below 1,000m (3,300ft) peaks.

The gateway to 25,000-acre Killarney National Park, where visitors can explore walking trails, glacially carved ridges, and lakes teeming with trout and salmon. Kayak the lakes of Killarney, or hike Carrauntoohil, Mangerton and MacGillycuddy's Reeks for spellbinding views.

Cork

Ireland's second largest city started as an island and now spans both sides of the River Lee. Expect a multitude of bridges.

The bustling market – which Rick Stein hailed as the "best covered market in the UK and Ireland" – is foodie heaven. There's a historic fort, Franciscan brewery, a French neo-Gothic masterpiece, old gaol, newer opera house, and even a butter museum!

"

I have never seen a
West Cork farmer
with an umbrella,
except at a funeral.

"

Damien Enright, *A Place Near Heaven –
A Year in West Cork*, 2004

Spike Island: Ireland's Alcatraz

Transformed from a 6th-century monastery to a grand fortress, and then to a prison, this island in Cork Harbour has a 1,300-year-old story, which is told in its public museum.

One of Europe's top attractions, it's a day trip from Cork city.

Kilkenny: "The Marble City"

Home to cobbled lanes and secret alleyways, castles and cathedrals, brewery tours and the best festivals.

Kilkenny was built with black limestone flecked with white seashells, hence the nickname, and Oliver Cromwell knocked down a wall of the 12th-century castle, which still dominates. Full of atmospheric pubs bursting with traditional music, Kilkenny is all about small-town charm with a big-city edge. It also has a vibrant creative scene.

Limerick

One of Ireland's oldest cities on the
River Shannon is a living museum,
with medieval castles and Georgian
splendour around every corner.

A city of secrets and stories, visitors rave
about its waterfront boardwalk, big gigs
and sporting events, stone circles and
artisan food at the Milk Market.

"

You might be poor,
your shoes might
be broken, but your
mind is a palace.

"

From Frank McCourt's memoir about a childhood
in Limerick, *Angela's Ashes*, 1996

Belfast

The capital and largest city in
Northern Ireland its ship-building, rope
and linen production may have passed, but
hip hotels, luxury apartments, world-class
musicians, shopping, gardens, Victorian
architecture, music-filled pubs and a
growing food and art scene are all thriving.

Titanic Museum Belfast

Located on the old Harland & Wolff shipyard where they built the super luxurious liner, this museum boasts nine galleries, multiple outdoor plazas, original artefacts, historic slipways, memorials, life-size outlines, an RMS *Titanic* tender ship and the last remaining White Star Line vessel in the world.

Castles

Ancient fortified homes for kings, chieftains or Anglo settlers, Ireland has over 30,0000 castles, located on rivers, headlands and hills throughout this ancient land. Moats, towers, turrets, dungeons, keeps, mullioned windows: yes, it's all here, so why not, take a tour, have a feast, even stay overnight!

The Rock of Cashel

Includes a 27m (90ft) round tower from the 1100s and a 12th-century chapel, as well as. Irish frescoes, Celtic art and Medieval architecture.

Bunratty Castle

Built on an ancient Viking trading camp in 970 AD, with collections of art, furniture, and tapestries from the 15th century.

The Wild Atlantic Way

At 2,500 km (1,550 miles) long,
this is the longest uninterrupted coastal
route in the world.

From Donegal in the north, all the way
down the west coast of Ireland to the
Old Head of Kinsale in the south, there are
panoramic views across epic landscapes,
deserted beaches, sheer cliffs and the
crashing Atlantic.

The Giant's Causeway

Sixty million years have fashioned
an incredible rock formation of basalt
columns on the beautiful Northern
Irish coastline.

According to the legend, it was created
by the Irish giant Finn McCool
(or Fionn Mac Cumhaill).

Dingle Peninsula

This peninsula on the south-west coast has been voted "the most beautiful place on earth" by *National Geographic*.

Dominated by the Slieve Mish mountain range, the Dingle Peninsula juts into the Atlantic, while its coastline of steep sea-cliffs, dramatic headlands and sandy beaches is dotted with lovely villages rich in tradition and culture.

Aran Islands

Three windswept treeless islands are home to "the most magnificent barbaric monument in Europe".

The 2,000-year-old Dun Aengus Fort, on the edge of a sheer 100m (325ft) cliff is an important archaeological site and is home to a truly spectacular view.

Cliffs of Moher

Every year over one million people visit
the Cliffs of Moher in County Clare.

At 214m (700ft) at their highest point, they
stretch 8km (5 miles) along the Atlantic
coast in the west of Ireland.

The Ring of Kerry

This 179km (110-mile) scenic drive
through rural seaside villages skirts
the coastline of the spectacular Iveragh
Peninsula, giving panoramic Atlantic
Ocean views across stunning islands, wild
sweeping mountains and ancient castles.

Croagh Patrick

One of Ireland's most famous and stunning mountain climbs near Westport in County Mayo.

On July's last Sunday, pilgrims climb Croagh Patrick in honour of Ireland's patron saint, who fasted and prayed on the summit for 40 days.

Slieve League Cliffs

One of Ireland's best-kept secrets, the 600m (1,970ft)-high cliffs tower over the sea, making them some of the highest sea cliffs in Europe!

It's a walk in the clouds, on the edge of the world.

Valley of Two Lakes

A day trip from Dublin, the lake of Glendalough is one of Ireland's best known monastic sites, located in the heart of the Wicklow Mountains National Park.

Newgrange

85m (279 feet) in diameter.
13m (42 feet) high.

A Stone Age monument in the Boyne Valley County Meath is one of Ireland's wonders. Dating back 5,200 years, it is older than Stonehenge and the Great Pyramids.

Immense round white stone walls domed in grass conceal an internal passageway leading to a chamber that illuminates at sunrise on the winter solstice.

Birding

Birdwatching is popular in Ireland. Observe the natural birdlife, then the winter migrations season from Europe and the Arctic.

In summer, a range of African birds are reported. See pintails, light-bellied brent geese, red-breasted mergansers, ringed plovers, snow buntings, sanderlings and short-eared owls.

Top Spots for the Birder

Rathlin Island, County Antrim:
Top RSPB Seabird Centre

Cape Clear Island, County Cork:
For Siberian and American rarities

**Castle Espie Wetland Centre,
County Down:** Home to Ireland's largest
collection of native and exotic birds

North Bull Island, Dublin:
For birdwatching with world-class status

**Lough Neagh Discovery and Conference
Centre, County Armagh:** Designated
National Nature Reserve

Chapter
THREE

Kick-offs & Throw-ins

Ireland is a sporting nation.
Whether it's indigenous, under-7's
or an international event, representing
village, town or city... sport is close
to a religion.

Full of calamities, broken dreams and
returns from the dead, requests for
divine intercession are not limited to
the pew, but take place at Irish sports
grounds across the country.

Hurling

Thousands of years old, also known as "The world's fastest game". Think airborne hockey, with aggressive contact and no time-outs. Or lacrosse with a few nips of whiskey. Think two teams of fifteen armed with heavy sticks munking a leather ball at goals 145 metres (475 feet) apart on a field 90 metres (295 feet) wide for 70 minutes.

Fast. Exhilarating. Fierce.

> **"**
>
> Several broken sticks, two broken heads, and two bruised fingers were part of the afternoon's play, for hurling, the Irish national game, is the fastest and probably the most dangerous of sports. It is a combination of hockey, football, golf, baseball, battle and sudden death. It was a real Irish game.
>
> **"**

Daily Mail, reporting on a match held in London (1921)

The All-Ireland Hurling Finale regularly makes the "Ten Sporting Events You Have to See Live" list. Croke Park attracts more than 82,000 spectators.

The ball hits speeds of 100mph. That's one-and-a-half times as fast as a baseball and one-and-one-third times as fast as a hurricane! Crowds are all in.

66

The toughest match I ever
heard of was the 1935 All-Ireland
Semi-Final. After 6 minutes, the
ball ricocheted off a post and
went into the stand. The pulling
continued relentlessly and it was
22 minutes before any of the
players noticed the ball
was missing.

99

Michael Smith, player for Tipperary

Gaelic Football: "The beautiful game"

Think football with hand balls, but without the whinging for penalties. Two teams of fifteen on a rectangular grass pitch, with H-shaped goals and a round leather ball. 1 point for over the bar, 3 points for under.

The ball is kicked, caught, hand-passed and punched… as are the players. Athleticism, speed, precision, chicanery, passion, skulduggery – this sport has it all.

"

Now listen, lads,
I'm not happy with
our tackling. We're
hurting them but they
keep getting up.

"

John B. Keane , Irish playright

Football: "The World Game"

The Irish love football and both pros and part-timers play. Although the English Premier League, along with Rangers and Celtic, is popular, try saying local rivalries don't mater.

The League of Ireland governs in the Republic, whereas it's the Irish League in Northern Ireland.

66

People always say I shouldn't be burning the candle at both ends. Maybe they haven't got a big enough candle.

99

George Best, as seen in Jack Beresford, "19 Iconic George Best Quotes", *Irish Post*, 28 September 2021

Rugby

Rugby is the third most popular sport in Ireland, and the national team is one of the best in the world. Leinster, Munster and Ulster are the leading provinces and have all won the European Champions Cup.

A full Aviva Stadium for an International is a once-in-a-lifetime experience for travellers.

66

Every kid grows up dreaming of
playing for Ireland. When you do
that the next thing you want to
do is win something for Ireland.
To win something as captain in
that special green jersey is what
dreams are made of.

99

Rory Best, Irish captain, after the team's Six Nations
triumph of 2018

Horse Racing

Ireland has a reputation for breeding and
training thoroughbreds.

A recurring part of Irish culture, the
horse has been romanticised in art and
literature for many centuries.

"

If it was one of
those soccer lads
they'd be down until
next Easter.

"

Ted Walsh on a jockey who took a heavy fall and kicking
in the Irish National

There are 27 racecourses throughout Ireland.

The National Hunt races run in the summer over hurdles and fences, while the summer months host the Flat.

Curragh Racecourse

Situated on the Curragh Plain, the Curragh is the most prestigious thoroughbred racecourse in Ireland and the home of all four Classics: the Irish Derby; Irish Oaks; Irish 2000 Guineas; and Irish 1000 Guineas.

The use of the Curragh as an early location for horse racing is mentioned in a 7th-century text.

Golf

With weather made for growing grass,
and over 400 clubs, golf is a major
participation sport in Ireland.

Home to 25% of all the natural links
courses in the world, it's safe to
say there's a huge amount of local
talent. May to September are the
bestmonths for a round, and there are
some exceptional courses in amazing
locations.

My favourite place to play golf is in Ireland. It's the most beautiful country to play golf in. And when you come as a guest, you're treated like a king.

Bill Murray

Royal County Down

Nestled in the Murlough Nature Reserve, flanked by the Mountains of Mourne and running along Dundrum Bay, Royal County Down is considered by many to be the most beautiful course in the world.

Revered, respected, worshipped – its narrow fairways and "bearded bunkers" provide a true test that rewards excellent control of the ball.

"

This is among my favourite places to play in Northern Ireland, one of the truly great links courses. The more you play it, the more you recognise it for the class place it is.

"

Rory McIlroy on Royal County Down

Road Bowling

Throw an 800-gram cast-iron ball along a public road for 1 or 2 kilometres in the least number of throws. Betting obligatory. There are 200 road bowling clubs in Cork alone!

Terms

Ball: bowl or bullet

Throw: shot

Butt: throwing mark

Breaking butt: stepping over the mark

Sop: grass marker where bowl must touch the road

"Faugh-a-Ballagh": "clear the way"

66

You can take a
man out of Ireland,
but you can't take
the Irishness out of
the man.

99

Tyson Fury

Chapter
FOUR

Single Malts, Burnt Barley & Sea Treats

With a climate that demands a warm hearth and a hearty meal, and social chat that requires elixirs to ease a dry throat, it makes sense that Ireland is home to gastronomic jewels now enjoyed the world over.

Craic

An essential Irish slang term describing a good time. The true meaning, however, embraces Irish culture and signifies something far greater, requiring great company and lively conversation, often accompanied by traditional Irish music.

Craic Levels

Good craic:
An Ok night out.

Mighty craic:
A fun night out.

Savage craic:
The Guinness was flowing, there were great jokes, even a chance of romance.

Deadly craic:
Such a memorable evening I can't tell you about it.

The craic was ninety:
A 5-star, mind-bogglingly awesome experience.

Drinking Etiquette

Ireland operates on the rounds system, whereby everyone takes a turn at buying drinks for the whole group. A shout should be returned and it is expected that the next round be bought before glasses are empty.

Irish Beer

With 5,000 years of brewing history (in monasteries, alehouses and homes, a rich soil and gentle rainfall producing quality barley, it's little wonder Ireland is famous for its beer.

While esteemed for its stout – its big names are global giants – a thriving small-batch craft-brewing scene is bringing new flavours to the tap.

66

The worst thing about
some men is that
when they are not
drunk they are sober.

99

W. B. Yeats

Irish Pubs

A drink is more than a glass, and a pub is more than a business. In Ireland, pubs are social spaces, community hubs, dance halls, a home for musical gatherings and touchstones to this country's culture and way of life.

Of course, connoisseurs of the black stuff and Irish whiskey are also catered for in such establishments.

Get to Know These...

Smithwick's Irish Ale
Approachable with a nice balance between malty and bitter flavours.

Harp Lager
Golden colour, low bitterness with a balance of malt and hops. Often paired with Guinness in a Half & Half.

Kilkenny
Malty notes, mild hop flavour, bubbles and creamy head.

"

Many people die of thirst, but the Irish are born with one.

"

Spike Milligan

Guinness: "The Black Stuff"

"Pint of gat": Ireland's staple alcoholic beverage ordered in its mother tongue.

Includes iron, antioxidants, liquid fibre, folate, ferulic acid, phytoestrogen, calcium and dietary silicon. It's said to lower cholesterol, and it's vegan to boot.

Black Velvet = Guinness + Champagne

Yes, you can!

A 20-ounce pint of Guinness only has
210 calories – that's less than a glass of
milk or orange juice!

Every batch at the Guinness factory
is taste-tested to ensure no bad batches
are sent out.

Pouring the Perfect Guinness

Use a Guinness-shaped pint glass.

Hold at a 45-degree angle.

Point the tap at the harp.

Fill.

Tip it up, even out, and leave some
room at the top.

Let it settle for 90 seconds.

When it's completely dark, top up, but
don't let the spout touch the stout.

Serve with the Guinness emblem
facing the customer.

The perfect pint of Guinness pours in 119.5 seconds.

66

The wine of Ireland.

99

James Joyce on Guinness stout

The Tall Blonde in a Black Dress is Well Travelled

Ireland is only the 3rd biggest consumer of Guinness.

Britain and Nigeria top the list.

Guinness is brewed in 49 countries and served in more than 150.

10 million glasses are poured daily.

Sláinte!

Traditional Irish toast meaning
"Good health".

Irish Whiskey

Whiskey is derived from the Gaelic term *"Uisce Beatha"*, which translates as "aqua vitae", or "water of life".

The first record of Irish whiskey dates back to 1405. From a local pastime, it evolved into an industry. By 1608, the Old Bushmills Distillery in Northern Ireland became the world's first licensed whiskey. Irish whiskey is revered for its smooth taste.

"
Whiskey is liquid sunshine.
"

George Bernard Shaw, Irish playwright

The Old Bushmills Distillery

At it since 1608, the oldest operating distillery, produces some of the finest whiskey in the world, namely, handcrafted triple-distilled whiskey in small batches. And although there is a premium tasting tour, it's not just for whiskey buffs.

Pay a visit to see how it's done.

Whiskey 101

Single-malt whiskeys
Made in a single distillery in pot stills from malted barley.

Single pot-still whiskeys
Made in a single distillery, in a pot still, from malted barley, unmalted barley and other grains.

Single-grain whiskeys
Made in a single distillery, but (confusingly) a mixture of cereals: malted barley (no more than 30%), unmalted barley, corn, or wheat.

Blended Irish whiskeys
Use a blend of at least two Irish whiskeys.

Food Pairings

Peated, heavily flavoured
Irish whiskeys go with fuller-flavoured
dishes such as:

Smoked salmon
Salty fish
Fatty red meats

Lighter, floral textured
Irish whiskeys go with lighter such as:

White meat
Canapés
Sushi

66

A good gulp of hot whiskey at bedtime – it's not very scientific, but it helps.

99

Alexander Fleming, Scottish inventor of penicillin

66

The light music
of whiskey falling
into a glass … an
agreeable interlude!

99

James Joyce

Some Classic
Irish Whiskey Cocktails

Irish Old-Fashioned

Irish Sour

Irish Whiskey Smash

Irish Mule

Irish coffee

Tipperary

Irish shot

Emerald

Dubliner

"

Only Irish coffee
provides in a single
glass all four essential
food groups: alcohol,
caffeine, sugar and fat.

"

Alex Levine

66

May the lilt of Irish laughter
lighten every load.

May the mist of Irish magic
shorten every road...

And may all your friends
remember all the favours
you are owed!

99

Irish toast

"

A good whiskey should be able
to hit you with a beautiful aroma
and engaging flavor. It should
be an experience that once
it touches your mouth, every
nerve in your body should be
screaming in order to fathom
what just happened.

"

Mario Petkovski, whiskyreviewer.com (2020)

Irish Food

Whether you're browsing a market showcasing the best local produce, picking favourites from an old-fashioned Irish menu, or sitting down for the meal of a lifetime in a restaurant in Dublin, Cork, Kilkenny or Galway, one thing is for certain: you'll not be losing weight in Ireland.

An Old-Fashioned Irish Menu

Here are some traditional dishes served in homes, pubs and restaurants across the country:

Soda bread
Sweetened with honey, seeded or flavoured with treacle and Guinness. Served warm and doused in butter.

Shellfish
Plump native oysters. Clams from Connemara. Cockles, mussels and Dublin Bay prawns.

Irish Stew
One-pot cooking with lamb, onions, herbs and potatoes.

Lough Neagh Eel
Northern Ireland specialty, served in wedges with white onion sauce.

Colcannon
A mash of potatoes, cabbage (or kale) and butter (or cream), flavoured with spring onions.

Boxty
A potato dumpling with bacon and eggs or smoked salmon and crème fraîche.

Boiled Bacon and Cabbage
Salted pork soaked overnight and then boiled with cabbage and potatoes, served with parsley sauce.

Coddle
Slow-cooked pork sausage and bacon, with sliced potatoes and onions.

Barmbrack
A fruity tea loaf, soaked in tea and whiskey, smothered in butter.

66

I'm Irish, so I'm used to odd stews. I can take it. Just throw a lot of carrots and onions in there, and I'll call it dinner.

99

Liam Neeson

Gone are the days when eating was jokingly referred to as penance in Ireland. A foodie revolution has meant innovative ex-patriate chefs and immigrants have brought imagination, new flavours and taste to quality local ingredients... pasture-grazed beef and lamb, award-winning dairy, abundant freshwater trout and salmon, as well as clean Atlantic fish and shellfish.

Irish Cheeses

In a country where grazing animals outnumber people, it's no surprise that Irish artisan cheesemakers are a talented bunch, offering a variety of styles.

Cashel blue: Tipperary's sweet, creamy, semi-firm blue.

Gubbeen: The "sticky toffee pudding of cheeses".

Killeen goat: Made using washed goats' curd, with nut and floral notes.

Cooleeney: An award-winning Camembert-style cheese.

Coolea: From a mountain farm in County Cork, gouda in style, with medium firmness, a buttery colour, and mild, sweet notes.

Milleens: A West Cork beauty with a firm, creamy texture, and a herbal, mushroomy, yet floral taste.

Corleggy: A hard handmade goat cheese with natural rind. Mild and nutty. Good with pinot noir.

Irish milk makes great ice cream, with unique flavours such as whiskey, sea salt and brown bread.

Pescatarian Heaven

With the Atlantic in the west and the Irish Sea in the east, wherever you sit down to eat in Ireland, you're never more than an hour's drive from the ocean. That means super-fresh seafood, including:

Fish pies, chowders, smoked kippers, and super fish and chips.

Crab cakes, cockles, scallops, prawns, smoked salmon and trout.

Pots of flavoursome steamed mussels straight from the sea to table.

Fresh oysters from Sligo County, perfect with just a squeeze of lemon and a pinch of salt.

Chapter
FIVE

Playing The Boot
&
Spilling Ink

The small population of a sea-locked island has produced some of the greatest 20th-century writers, Nobel prize-winners, trailblazing literary giants and a stream of contemporary writers and poets.

Is it something in the beer?

Commas and Full-stops

From inscriptions cut into wood and stone to modern-day masterpieces, Ireland has had a great literary tradition for over 1,000 years. It has made massive contributions to poetry, drama, and the form known as the English novel, as well as producing a whole host of genre-defying pioneers.

Why? No one knows for sure, but Ireland's high literacy rates, a penchant for experimentation, a zest for language, curiosity and a national love of storytelling all hold clues.

> **66**
>
> # Words are the clothes thoughts wear.
>
> **99**

Samuel Beckett

Irish Nobel Laureates in Literature

W. B. Yeats

George Bernard Shaw

Samuel Beckett

Seamus Heaney

"

I've always associated the
moment of writing with
a moment of lift, of joy, of
unexpected reward.

"

Seamus Heaney

Irish Booker Prize-Winners

Roddy Doyle – *Paddy Clarke Ha Ha Ha*

John Banville – *The Sea*

Anne Enright – *The Gathering*

"

I want to tell my daughters,
each time you fall in love it is
important, even at nineteen...
if you can, at nineteen, count the
people you love on one hand, you
will not, at forty, have run out of
fingers on the other.

"

Anne Enright, *The Gathering* , 2007

Great Irish Reads 1

Ulysses – James Joyce

The Picture of Dorian Gray – Oscar Wilde

Amongst Women – John McGahern

The Last September – Elizabeth Bowen

Gulliver's Travels – Jonathan Swift

Dracula – Bram Stoker

Star of the Sea – Joseph O'Connor

The Country Girls – Edna O'Brien

The Lion, the Witch, and the Wardrobe – C. S. Lewis

66

You can never get
a cup of tea large
enough or a book long
enough to suit me.

99

C. S. Lewis

Great Irish Reads 2

The Commitments – Roddy Doyle

Brooklyn – Colm Tóibín

Milkman – Anna Burns

Angela's Ashes – Frank McCourt

The Importance of Being Earnest –
Oscar Wilde

Dubliners – James Joyce

A Girl Is a Half-Formed Thing –
Eimear McBride

The Butcher Boy – Patrick McCabe

Normal People – Sally Rooney

The Pull of the Stars – Emma Donoghue

Borstal Boy – Brendan Behan

Be yourself; everyone else is already taken.

Oscar Wilde

James Joyce

One of the most innovative and influential writers of the 20th century, Joyce's technical innovations, experimental prose and mastery of language made him a seminal figure of modernism.

Ulysses, with its depth of character, breadth of humour, stream-of-consciousness narration, and frankness regarding human nature, was either a masterpiece or incomprehensible.

"

Her antiquity in preceding and surviving succeeding tellurian generations: her nocturnal predominance: her satellitic dependence: her luminary reflection: her constancy under all her phases, rising and setting by her appointed times, waxing and waning: the forced invariability of her aspect: her indeterminate response to inaffirmative interrogation: her potency over effluent and refluent waters: her power to enamour, to mortify...

"

James Joyce, *Ulysses*

Bloomsday

June 16th, the day the book
Ulysses took place, is observed
annually in Dublin and around
the world.

People Celebrate James Joyce by:

Reading sections of Ulysses (or the whole book!)

Visiting the places mentioned in the book.

Eating the same breakfast as Leopold Bloom consumed: Irish breakfast with fried pork kidney and liver.

66

He wanted to cry quietly but not for himself: for the words, so beautiful and sad, like music.

99

A Portrait of the Artist as a Young Man, James Joyce, 1916

"

Being Irish, he had an
abiding sense of tragedy,
which sustained him
through temporary
periods of joy.

"

W. B. Yeats

Modern Irish Literary Giants

William Trevor: "The greatest living writer of short stories in English", *New Yorker*

Ann-Enright: Booker Prize-winner

John Banville: "I'm one of those writers who dislikes and is shamed by his own work".

Roddy Doyle: Booker Prize-winner

Joseph O'Connor: Novelist, screenwriter, playwright and broadcaster

Maeve Binchy: Has sold 40 million copies of her books in 37 languages

Colum McCann: "The best writers attempt to become alternative historians."

66

The heart of an
Irishman is nothing
but his imagination.

99

George Bernard Shaw

Ireland On Screen

Breathtaking landscapes and skilled crews
make Ireland a favourite place for filmmakers to
continue the tradition of storytelling. Some you
may know include:

The Crying Game	*Killing Bono*
In the Name of the Father	*Finding You*
Michael Collins	*Sing Street*
Once	*My Left Foot*
The Guard	*Ryan's Daughter*
The Commitments	*Far and Away*
Ripper Street	*The Long Good Friday*
PS I Love You	*Waking Ned Devine*
Braveheart	*Vikings*
Belfast	*Game of Thrones*

66

Ireland was a place
for the renewal of
hope and I still see
it like that.

99

Daniel Day-Lewis

Music

Ireland has given the world more than its fair
share of singers and players.
Here's a few you may have listened to:

The Coors	Them
The Boomtown Rats	Liam O'Flynn
The Pogues	Paddy Keenan
Thin Lizzy	The Chieftans
The Cranberries	The Fureys
Horslips	Van Morrison
Westlife	Enya
U2	Sinéad O'Connor
My Bloody Valentine	Damien Rice
Flogging Molly	Boyzone
Snow Patrol	Hozier
Stiff Little Fingers	The Script
The Undertones	

> **"**
> Music keeps
> the heart porous in
> many ways.
> **"**

Bono

Ireland is the only country in the world to have a musical instrument as its national emblem.

The harp.

"

For you can't hear Irish
tunes without knowing
you're Irish and wanting
to pound that fact into
the floor.

"

Jennifer Armstrong, *Becoming Mary Mehan*, 2002

Traditional Irish Music

Whether it's open mics, traditional gigs, Irish instruments, pavement buskers, spontaneous sessions, or nightly entertainment, there's a hundred different ways to get in tune with Ireland's love of music.

The traditional Irish music pouring from the pubs, and flowing through the streets is played on these unique instruments.

Melodeon: A basic button accordion

Concertina: A free-reed instrument, similar to an accordion

Uilleann pipes: Similar to bagpipes

Harp: A staple of Irish traditional music

Bodhrán: A goatskin drum

Banjo: A stringed instrument resembling a guitar

Tin or Penny Whistle: A six-hole, two-octave woodwind instrument

Fiddle: Similar to a violin

Playing the boot: Another name for foot-tapping

"

Irish music is guts, balls and feet music, yeah? It's frenetic dance music, yeah? Or it's impossibly sad like slow music, yeah? Yeah? And it also handles all sorts of subjects, from rebel songs to comical songs about sex, you know what I mean, yeah?

"

Shane MacGowan, Irish singer-songwriter

"

I started hitching about the country when I was 16 or 17 years old. I found the music that was played around the country – Irish music – had a particular resonance.

"

Brendan Gleeson

Bodhrán: "The pulse of Irish music"

Goatskins are soaked in lime and secret ingredients for 7 to 10 days before being stretched, then tacked onto a steamed birch hoop.

The skin stays taught for a lifetime and has a deep, haunting tone.

Irish Harp

The triangular framed cláirseach has
30 to 50 highly tensioned brass strings and
a resonating chamber carved from a single
piece of willow.

Plucked with fingernails, it produces a
ringing bell-like sound. Ireland's unique
national emblem appears on coins as well
as the Coat of Arms.

Irish Tin Whistle

This ancient and enduring instrument is not just a toy. In the right, hands this flute makes the most expressive, energetic and lilting sound.

Accessible, portable, with six front finger holes, just remember to blow gently and keep your fingers light.

Uilleann Pipes

A set of bellows strapped round the waist are worked by the arm, sending air through the chanter, drones and regulators.

With a two-octave range, these pipes are played sitting down. They have harmonics, a sweeter sound and are quieter than other bagpipes.

Irish Dancing 101

Dancing is a feature of Irish traditional music. Native traditional folk dances have been important for centuries as a way of socialising, protesting and affirming national identity.

Shoes depend on the style of dance. Male Flat Down step dancers have metal cleats on their toes and heels, whereas Ballet Up dance shoes have soft soles.

"

And the merry love
the fiddle, and the
merry love to dance.

"

W. B. Yeats

Yes, you can!

Irish dancing is physically demanding of the core, hips and ankles, requires attention to detail and a high amount of skill.

There's tons of dance academies where kids as young as three start to learn, but it's never too late to start. Progress through beginner, advanced beginner, novice and championship levels.

"

I dance because there's no greater feeling in the world than moving to a piece of music and letting the rest of the world disappear.

"

Ciara Sexton, five-time World and All-Ireland
Irish dance champion

Irish Dance Styles

Ceili: A native Irish dance to quadrilles, reels, jigs, long or round

Sean-nós: An older style, often solo

Irish Two-Handed Dancing: Couples dance in specific patterns

Traditional Irish Step Dancing: Males and females in lines, circles, squares or partnered reels

Modern Irish Step Dance: Females perform Ballet up movements, while the males shoe-tap

Irish Set Dancing: Couples dance in four sets

Riverdance

Performed by Michael Flatley and Jean Butler in the seven-minute interval of Eurovision 1994, *Riverdance* has since taken the world by storm.

With a mesmerising soundtrack (composed by Bill Whelan) and ground-breaking visuals, 25 years later it has become one of the most internationally recognized stage shows of all time.

66

I'm proud of my Irish
heritage and culture and
this show will feature a lot
of Irish dancing.

99

Michael Flatley, creator of *Riverdance,*
Lord of the Dance and Feet of Flames

An Old Irish Blessing

May the road rise up to meet you.

May the wind always be at your back.

May the sun shine warm upon your face,
and rains fall soft upon your fields.

And until we meet again, may God hold
you in the palm of His hand.

Chapter
SIX

Far & Wide

Empty stomachs, gold rushes,
religious freedom, family ties and
opportunity have lured Ireland's
people to all corners of the globe.

The Great Hunger

The Irish Potato Famine was a period of starvation when the crop was destroyed by blight. Roughly a million died.

Between 1845 and 1855, 2.1 million people emigrated in one of the greatest exoduses in history. Greater freedoms and chances of success meant emigrations continued across generations.

"

You've got to think lucky. If you fall into a mudhole, check your back pocket – you might have caught a fish.

"

Darrell Royal, American football player and coach

True That

5 million people live in Ireland.

80 million people with Irish
heritage live abroad!

> **"**
> That's what the holidays
> are for – for one person to
> tell the stories and another
> to dispute them. Isn't that
> the Irish way?
> **"**

Lara Flynn Boyle as seen on Bustle.com

Where are they now?

The number of people claiming Irish descent by percentage of the population in other countries around the world:

Irish American	33,348,049	11%
Irish British	14,000,000	10%
Irish Canadian	4,554,870	14%
Irish Australian	7,000,000	30%
Irish Scots	100,000	18%
Irish Argentinian	1,000,000	3%

Do You Know These Irish Americans?

Walt Disney

Barack Obama

Eileen Marie Collins

Gene Kelly

Bruce Springsteen

Michael Flatley

Kurt Cobain

Henry Ford

John and Jackie Kennedy

Billy the Kid

Festivals Celebrated by Irish Communities Around the World

St. Patrick's Day

St. Stephen's Day (Feast of Saint Stephen)

Samhain Festival (The Irish Halloween)

May Day (The International Workers' Day/ Labour Day)

The Rose of Tralee International Festival

Galway International Arts Festival (GIAF)

Summer Solstice (Midsummer)

The Winter Solstice

Irish Whiskey Day

> The list of Irish saints is past counting; but in it all no other figure is so human, friendly, and lovable as St. Patrick.

Stephen Gwynn

Their National Day Goes With Them

St Patrick's Day, the Irish National Holiday, celebrated every 17 March, is marked across the globe.

It's been celebrated from the Molly Blooms pub in Israel to outer space, from Montserrat to Buenos Aires, from Tokyo to Singapore, from Mumbai to Dubai, from Moscow to Oslo.

> **"**
> For the whole
> world is Irish on the
> Seventeenth o' March!
> **"**

Thomas Augustine Daly, Irish-American poet

St. Patrick's Day

St. Patrick was a Roman that arrived in
Ireland as a boy slave. After six years, he
escaped, thanking his faith in God for
helping him gain freedom.

March 17 commemorates the missionary
Saint Patrick and the arrival of
Christianity in Ireland. It celebrates the
heritage, people, art, religion and culture
of the Irish.

St. Patrick's Day in Chicago is one of the biggest. The river is dyed emerald green. There's a parade of floats, full of firefighters, social and cultural clubs, police, Irish step dancers, and bands. Wherever you celebrate, expect elves, fairies and dancing, as well as the odd leprechaun. The day starts with an Irish breakfast at the pub, and after the parade, the party is just getting started.

St. Patrick's Day is the closest thing in America to National Immigrant Day, a tribute not only to the Irish, but to the idea that Americans are all part "other".

"

If you're Irish, it doesn't matter where you go – you'll find family.

"

Victoria Smurfit, Irish actress